U.S. SYMBOLS   WITHDRAWN

THE STAR-SPANGLED BANNER

by Tyler Monroe

Consulting Editor: Gail Saunders-Smith, PhD

CAPSTONE PRESS
a capstone imprint

Pebble Plus is published by Capstone Press,
1710 Roe Crest Drive, North Mankato, Minnesota 56003
www.capstonepub.com

Library of Congress Cataloging-in-Publication Data
Monroe, Tyler.
  The star-spangled banner / by Tyler Monroe.
  pages cm.—(Pebble Plus. U.S. Symbols)
  Includes bibliographical references and index.
  Summary: "Simple text and full-color photographs briefly describe "The Star-Spangled Banner" and its role as a national symbol"—Provided by publisher.
  ISBN 978-1-4765-3087-1 (library binding)—ISBN 978-1-4765-3509-8 (ebook pdf) — ISBN 978-1-4765-3536-4 (pbk.)
1. Baltimore, Battle of, Baltimore, Md., 1814—Juvenile literature. 2. Star-spangled banner (Song)--Juvenile literature.
3. National songs—United States—History and criticism—Juvenile literature 4. Key, Francis Scott, 1779-1843—Juvenile literature. I. Title.
E356.B2M66 2014
782.42'15990973—dc23   2013001824

Editorial Credits
Erika L. Shores, editor; Lori Bye, designer; Svetlana Zhurkin, media researcher; Eric Manske, production specialist

Photo Credits
Alamy: North Wind Picture Archives, 9; Corbis: Smithsonian Institution, 19; Dreamstime: Catabar, 7; Getty Images: AFP/ Mark Ralston, 21; Library of Congress, cover, 11, 13, 15, 17; Shutterstock: Eric Broder Van Dyke, 1, Jose Gil, 5, Suat Gursozlu (stars), cover and throughout

Note to Parents and Teachers

The U.S. Symbols set supports national social studies standards related to people, places, and culture. This book describes and illustrates the Star-Spangled Banner. The images support early readers in understanding the text. The repetition of words and phrases helps early readers learn new words. This book also introduces early readers to subject-specific vocabulary words, which are defined in the Glossary section. Early readers may need assistance to read some words and to use the Table of Contents, Glossary, Read More, Internet Sites, and Index sections of the book.

Printed in China by Nordica.
0413/CA21300494
032013   007226NORDF13

TABLE OF CONTENTS

A National Song

People around the world sing songs that praise their countries. Many of these songs are national anthems. "The Star-Spangled Banner" is the U.S. national anthem.

The Star-Spangled Banner

O say can you see, by the dawn's early light,
What so proudly we hailed at the twilight's last gleaming?
Whose broad stripes and bright stars through the perilous fight,
O'er the ramparts we watched were so gallantly streaming?
And the rocket's red glare, the bombs bursting in air,
Gave proof through the night that our flag was still there,
O say does that star-spangled banner yet wave
O'er the land of the free and the home of the brave?

5

"The Star-Spangled Banner" stands for courage and respect. Americans showed courage when the song was written. Singing the song today shows respect for the United States.

The Attack on Fort McHenry

During the War of 1812, Francis Scott Key went to help a friend. His friend was being held on a British ship near Baltimore, Maryland.

Key was kept on the ship while the British attacked nearby Fort McHenry on September 13, 1814. The next morning Key saw the American flag still flying over the fort.

A Poem Becomes a Song

The Americans had won the battle.

Key felt proud to be an American.

He wrote a poem about the fight

and the flag. He called it

"The Defense of Fort McHenry."

the home of the brave?

On the shore dimly seen through the mists of the de[ep]
Where the foe's haughty host in dread silence repos[es]
What is that which the breeze, o'er the towering steep,
As it fitfully blows, half conceals, half discloses?
Now it catches the gleam of the morning's first beam
In full glory reflected now shines in the stream,
'Tis the star-spangled banner — O long may it wave
O'er the land of the free & the home of the brave!

And where is that band who so vauntingly swore,
That the havoc of war & the battle's confusion
A home & a Country should leave us no more?
Their blood has wash'd out their foul footstep's pollution
No refuge could save the hireling & slave
From the terror of flight or the gloom of the grave,
And the star-spangled banner in triumph doth
[O]'er the land of the free & the [home of the brave]

13

A newspaper in Baltimore printed
Key's poem. Some time later
people added music to the poem.
The song became known as
"The Star-Spangled Banner."

The song became popular in the late 1800s. The U.S. military sang it when raising and lowering the flag. It became the official U.S. anthem in 1931.

The Symbol Today

The flag that flew at Fort McHenry

in 1814 is also called the

Star-Spangled Banner. Today

it is found in a museum in our

nation's capital, Washington, D.C.

At events, Americans sing or play

"The Star-Spangled Banner."

People sing it before sports events.

It's played at the Olympic Games

when Americans win gold medals.

20

Glossary

courage—bravery in times of danger

fort—a building that is well defended against attacks

military—the armed forces of a country

national anthem—a national song

Olympic Games—a competition of many sports events held every four years in a different country; people from around the world compete against each other

praise—words telling someone he or she did a good job

respect—a feeling that shows you value someone or something

War of 1812—a war between the United States and Great Britain; it lasted from 1812 to 1815

Read More

Harris, Nancy. *National Anthem.* Patriotic Symbols. Chicago: Heinemann Library, 2008.

Pearl, Norman. *Our National Anthem.* American Symbols. Minneapolis: Picture Window Books, 2007.

Wesolowski, Harriet. *The Songs We Sing: Honoring Our Country.* I'm an American Citizen. New York: PowerKids Press, 2013.

Internet Sites

FactHound offers a safe, fun way to find Internet sites related to this book. All of the sites on FactHound have been researched by our staff.

Here's all you do:

Visit *www.facthound.com*

Type in this code: 9781476530871

Super-cool stuff! Check out projects, games and lots more at www.capstonekids.com

Critical Thinking Using the Common Core

1. Why did Francis Scott Key write "The Star-Spangled Banner"?
   (Key Ideas and Details)

2. Describe how Key's poem turned into our national anthem.
   (Key Ideas and Details)

3. When and where do people often sing "The Star-Spangled Banner"?
   (Key Ideas and Details)

Index

Word Count: 242
Grade: 1
Early-Intervention Level: 22